Succession

Succession

POEMS BY
MARY SWANDER

Athens
The University of Georgia Press

Copyright © 1979 by the University of Georgia Press
Athens 30602

Set in 10 on 12 point Monticello type
Printed in the United States of America

Library of Congress Cataloging in Publication Data

Swander, Mary.
  Succession: poems.
  I. Title.
PS3569.W253S9   811'.5'4   79–12392
ISBN 0–8203–0479–4
ISBN 0–8203–0486–7 pbk.

for Rita Lynch Swander

Acknowledgments

The author and the publisher gratefully acknowledge permission to reprint the following poems which originally appeared in the publications here noted.

"From an Album" and "Lynching, 1493" (here slightly revised as section 2 of "Lynch's Window"), *Antioch Review;* "Succession" (here titled "Sweater") and "This House," *Cut Bank;* "Swift," *Iowa Review;* "Folding Up," "Needlepoint," "Shell," and "Winter, 1975," *The Nation;* "Sweater" (here titled "Succession"), *Ohio Review;* "In a Dream," "Letter" (here slightly revised and titled "Cloud"), and "Song," *Poetry;* "For Marcus Lynch," *Ploughshares;* "Quay," *Missouri Review;* "Currach" and section 1 of "Lynch's Window," *Portland Review.*

"Dutton's Place," "Folding Up," "In a Dream," "Needlepoint," "November," "Song," "Succession," "Sweater," and "This House" appeared in *Needlepoint,* a chapbook (Smokeroot Press, Cut Bank editions, University of Montana, 1977).

Contents

"*There are some creatures that do not seem to die at all; they simply vanish totally into their own progeny. Single cells do this. The cell becomes two, then four, and so on, and after a while the last trace is gone.*"

Lewis Thomas, *The Lives of a Cell*

I
Lynch's Window

In 1493 in Galway, Ireland, Walter Lynch confessed to the murder of a man named Gomez. The year before, Walter's father, the Lord Mayor Lynch, had brought the Spaniard back from a trading venture and apprenticed him into the family business. At this time Walter was engaged to a woman named Anne, and after seeing Gomez leave her house several times late at night, Walter stabbed him, then floated the body out into the bay. In the morning, when the corpse washed up on shore, Walter's plumed hat was found nearby and became the chief piece of evidence at the trial.

Walter's father, as magistrate and judge, found he could only convict and condemn his son to death by hanging and so ordered the execution. Several weeks before, the pope had sent him a crystal rosary to give him the strength to make the conviction. But no one in the town would carry out the order, and Walter remained for months locked in a prison cell in his father's own castle. Finally, the mayor brought a priest into the room to hear Walter's confession, then strung a rope from the ceiling beam, embraced his son as he slipped a noose around his neck and, while Anne wept outside below, pushed Walter out the window.

Later, the townspeople chiseled a small head of Death into the castle wall just below the window. Soon after, the father died of grief, and since that time individual beads of the rosary have been found in scattered parts of the country.

Lynch's Window

1

There is a son kneeling
on a stone floor,
a father standing
at the window,

a priest beside him.
This is a last confession.
There is a son
telling his story.

He stabbed the man
three times in the heart
then floated the body
out into the bay.

And now it has all
come back to this: a rope
tied from the ceiling beam,
a cloud at the window,

blocking the light,
beads of rain just
beginning to form
on the castle wall,

the son's features
a blur, his eyes closed,
as a cloth falls
over his face,

as his father draws
him close against
his chest, the priest's
hands opening in a final

blessing over this:
a single cell:
house of the father,
flesh of the son.

2

There is a plumed hat
lying on a stone floor,
its feathers arching
toward the window,

a small skull
beneath the window
freshly chiseled
into stone.

It's beginning to rain.
There is the rope,
the ceiling beam,
the plumed hat

found near the body
washed from the bay,

the sword left
in the sand,

the crystal rosary
sent by the pope
to give the father strength.
And there is the father

standing in the room,
the rosary in his hand.
Its dark amber beads
shine in the dim light.

They swing down, tighten,
become heavy with weight.
They swing down, snap
and break, falling

through the air,
falling like feathers,
dissolving in the rain,
into lead, into sand.

Cloud

There are waves here
breaking into splinters
like smashed glass
upon the rocks

There are lines and
creases on the rocks
A man swimming near
the shore looks at them

then is gone again
There is a fish
its fin shaped like
a sword rises on

a wide blank sea
It's a dark day
There is a cloud
here that hangs

in the air and
droops like a flag
in valediction
There is a woman

She sits there and
smiles and smiles
with her hand on
the tiller of the moon

Quay

The boat is waiting
far out in the harbor.
There is a man on board,
leaning over the railing,
a woman standing on the dock,
her black shawl wrapped
around her shoulders,
her head, her red petticoat
showing just beneath her knees.
She is not weeping.
She is not even waving.
Her small white handerchief
is tucked into her sleeve.
She does not wait
to watch the mast
disappear into the sea.
She does not huddle
together with the other women
like the swans
trying to squeeze
the first bit of morning
heat from the rocks
on the shore.
She turns and walks on
past the market where
the pig's knuckles
and black and white puddings
are packed in ice,
and the fish scales
glow purple as small coals.

There she stops and
blows on her hands.
She looks back.
Along the bay she sees
horses running wild
among the cattle,
boys in blue shirts
playing with a ball
along the sand.
A dog trots
across the horizon.
The daffodils and whinbush
are just flowering.
There is the smell of peat
burning, blackening the chimneys.
The grass is very green.

Galway, Ireland

For Mary Lynch

The white cement walls, thatched roof,
the rose bush blooming just outside, the small table
inside next to your rocker—it all looked so familiar.

And over the hearth, the picture of the Virgin's heart,
the layers of flesh torn away, the bramble
of thorns twisted around the fist-shaped muscle.

And the picture of your father, his fields
dried up, the potatoes shriveled to the size
of your fingers, then curled back into the earth,

everyone else gone and relatives
there at the tip of Inishmore, "the isle of tears,"
taking one last look at the ships leaving.

That night I found you in the old church
kneeling alone, hands folded, your white hair
wet with rain, pressed under a woolen scarf,

the soft light of the votive candle blurring
your face, and I could feel the weight of your body,
of a whole family, fall away, dissolve as if a thin wafer.

The next morning we ate breakfast together:
eggs, scones, tea, brown bread and strawberry jam.
Then half way down the road, I turned and waved,

the ship's bell clanging. You stood there by the bush,
the sun shining into the house, your one hand
raised, the fingers, blossoms, curled open.

For Marcus Lynch

A man enters the room,
a doctor,
who has my mother's
dark hair.
He moves closer
under the light.
I can smell his clean
starched shirt,
the sleeves rolled up,
the collar button loose.
I can see my face
in the mirror
tied to his forehead,
the light in my eyes.
He sits on the bed,
speaks with a thick brogue
and says something
hard for me to understand.
He tells of old nuns
settling on a bench
at night,
warm under their long habits,
drawing in their rosaries
like ropes from a boat leaving.
He tells of a woman
on the west coast of Ireland,
spinning, winding yarn
around her husband's arms.
The yarn rolls into a ball,
slips to the floor, hardens

into a small stone head,
the man's face dark, severe.
He stands at the foot
of my bed and nods.
Then nothing can save me,
not the doctor
feeding me herbs,
walking toward the door,
not even the old nuns
in the corner of the room,
unpinning their veils.
The cloth falls
in front of my eyes,
and grandfather, I call,
grandfather. I want him
to come back, to lift me up.
I want him to hold me, tightly,
my arms around his neck.

Scales

I slide the weights to the right,
the bar suspends in air,
then once again you are
in the room, dust in your sleeves,
your shoes covered with sand,
your black bag opening,
filling like a pool,
the only hint of water
in this dry summer.
The scales tip and I slide
down through the bag,
the floor, the cracked ground.
My body floats into a bay,
the waves lapping the rocks,
the gulls circling. A man
kneels, kisses the sand,
kisses the damp stones
of a castle room, a rope
tied from the ceiling beam.
He stands, teeters from one leg
to the other and the veins
in the stones flow together
forming the lines of a map.
He holds a compass in his hand.
The rope breaks and the room
floats west. The scales tip
back and I stand before the window,
your bag in my hand. Grandfather,
this is what you brought;
this is what you left:

scales, rags, needles,
your rosary, plumed hat and sword.
I stand before the window,
the light blaring, almost
blinding, the clouds folding,
shriveling to small metal balls.

II
This House

Needlepoint

1

Midnight,
my great-grandmother, Anna,
making rounds from house to house,

walking the back country roads
of Iowa: magician, mid-wife, nurse.
And I watch her enter one large room,

the water on the stove, the steam
rising, parting like a pair of legs,
the skin circling a wound. She holds

her daughter, and her daughter, by the heels,
the same disease winding through them,
the birth stains still on the bed.

She waves a needle in the air, a wand.
And stepping out again, she drags
a cauldron to the middle of the lawn

and marks the house with an X.
She stops. She strips by the gate,
boiling her dress after each new death.

2

When I was ten I found that dress
in the attic and wore it for Halloween.
I rode through the town on a broom,

Anna's arms, her hips matching mine,
her skirt gathered at my waist,
the neck twisted, tied in a knot.

At fifteen, I buried her daughter,
marking the place with a cross.
I remember the grave opening, closing,

the sun swaying in the sky, hanging
by a single thread. At twenty,
I buried her daughter. The priest

stood on the same spot, the ground
receiving his blessing, the canopy
flying over the same scene, the roses,

the acolytes in white holding the censer,
the incense rising like steam, falling
over my head like a piece of black cloth.

Sweater

I slip into your dress.
The cuffs close
around my wrists.

The collar lies
on my chest,
a thick vein.

Now I'm in your hats,
coats, gloves, each one
folding back into my body.

I slip into your blouse,
the buttons dissolving,
the buttons, black tears.

The threads unravel,
crawl into my arms,
spin dark

green cocoons.
Just beneath my skin,
wings are beating.

I slip into your sweater.

This House

1

I see my mother
on the porch sewing.

The thread winds around
her finger and tries to forget.

The needle sticks her finger
and her finger does not bleed.

Her hands have no feeling.
They move through the dark

like indigo buntings
on a fall night.

They navigate by the stars.
They find their way home

in the spring when the red oak
in the yard turns green.

The red oak in the yard
turns green, turns red.

The branches droop,
sweep across the porch.

The leaves fall, stabbing
tiny holes in the snow.

2

I hear my mother
in the kitchen singing.

She loses her place.
She loses her breath.

She places her hand over the stove
and the stove steams.

The stove swims toward her.
Her apron flaps

at her waist like a fin.
Her body slackens and shivers.

Her arms rise
and her body stiffens.

She floats through the door,
through other rooms.

She swims back
to the stream of her birth.

3

I see my mother
on the basement stairs

carrying a laundry basket
braced against her hip
as if it were a child.

It is Monday.
It is always Monday.

The old Maytag
chugs and spits.

The cement floor cracks
and the water drains from the tub.

The soap separates—
a slab of fat,
lye leached from ashes.

The clothes curl,
roll into a ball.

The whole cellar
goes into torpor.

4

I hear my mother
in the attic hunting
for her winter coat.

A trunk opens.
Daylight burrows in,
darkens.

My mother's coat hangs
in the corner, its arms
tucked under like wings.

My mother's coat hangs
from her body.
She sways.

She stoops.
She slumps to the floor.
She nestles under an eave,

draws her legs up to her chin,
crawls into herself,
buries her face in fur.

5

I sit on the stoop,
Mother, watching

the moon emerge, molt,
glide home,

move through the rooms
of this house,

rooms becoming
red and swollen.

Under the windows
the snow melts

exposing the sun,
an unlettered stone.

The sun rising
over this house,

spins, turns north,
waits for you

to return,
or take wing,

glide toward the moon,
glide home.

Dutton's Place

Nine p.m.
Night folds
its wings into the house.
My grandmother sits on the edge

of her bed and unwinds her hair.
She wheezes. She stares into the mirror
as if it would open like a window
and she might catch her breath.

But all the windows are shut,
the cracks stuffed and sealed
and there is nothing in the mirror,
no one in the room but me, sitting

on my grandmother's bed, her hair
woven into the quilt, the stitches
fraying, the flowers leaning into
themselves, toward the only light.

And now my mother moves from the
window where the plastic flaps against
the glass like the skin under her arm.
My mother lies down on the bed

and I lie with her. We pull the quilt
to our chins, let go our dream.
My grandmother's face glides over
our field, the flowers slowly closing,

as I tuck my head under my mother's arm,
listen to the valves, the doors
of her heart slide open, shut,
echo throughout the walls of the house.

In the next room the cat hears
the noise and stirs in her sleep.
There is a fur ball burning
inside her like the stone

warmed on the stove, wrapped in
flannel and placed at my feet.
My feet move, arch around the stone,
my body curls, slipping away,

sinking, like something drowning,
the walls falling in, falling with
me, the whole house collapsing
deep inside the ground like a lung.

Winter, 1975

These are the bare beams with the nails
showing through, the attic, the enclosed porch,
the closet where the cat had her first litter.

These are my grandmother's rooms, the kitchen,
the flour bin, the cupboard, the dish
where she soaked her teeth, the hole

she knocked in the wall for a window.
This is the space between the slats, the blinds,
the yellow light coming through, the dust beam,

the dust on the landing, the backstairs
that lead to the basement, the root-cellar,
the cache-pit, the place where my grandmother

buried her turnips, carrots, and beets.
There is the smell of wood chips, kerosene,
and an old load of coal dumped against

the rough white stone. There are two shelves
full of Mason jars along the wall,
the feel of the furnace heat, the cold dirt floor.

And here everything stops: the peaches up in
the air behind blue glass—underground,
the tuber with its flesh, its whole skin, stays.

Pegasus

I lie back on the porch swing.
She is inside, beyond the bay window,
her hands scaling the piano keys.
To drink at the billa-bong, she sings
and the pedals creak louder in answer
to the locusts drumming against the screen.
This is a dry summer. Dust on the cushion,
dust on the railing, and no clouds in sight.
Now she moves further inside,
the music, the light, growing dimmer.
I lie back and watch the fireflies circle
the porch lamp, become a constellation.
The piano pedals ease and the music stops.
Through the hot August night, a lid, a wing, falls.

From an Album

Easter and the morning light shines
through my mother's wide-brimmed hat,
leaving her forehead in shadow.
My hat pushed farther back, tied
under the chin. The storm windows
still on, the grass brown, the bush
beside the porch not yet in full bloom,
but already my mother's face is thin,
her hair drawn up in a tight bun,
her hand on my shoulder, a twig,
a thorn, a bud breaking.

My grandmother and I on the front
lawn, squinting into the sun.
My grandmother's cheeks puffed,
flesh sagging over her knees.
The lines and creases on her face
matching those in the house behind
us. My grandmother's arm wrapped
around me, holding, propping me up
in the air, my shoulder locked into
hers, her elbow bent like a hinge.

Icicles hanging from the eaves,
the cottonwood. The elms in the
back yard going bad. One cut down,
stacked against the fence, the smoke
circling the chimney.
And me at the window, the snow piled
in drifts, sealing up the cracks

in the door. The odor of blue spruce
and pine. The tiny white lights
strung on the evergreen, blinking off
and on, off and on again and on.

Music and my mother at the piano
playing. My grandmother and I
on the couch, her song, her features
a blur in the tangle of white hair,
her head leaning back into the silk
slipcover. My head in her lap, falling
into the soft folds of her dress, her thighs,
the slipcover rising above me, blossoming
toward the ceiling, a snowcloud, a canopy
flying over our house, with no one, nothing
inside: no streamers, handles, ripcord.

Swift

Now it is loose in the room, ashes falling
from its wings, falling from the ceiling,
the large black flakes, the large black
wings pressed against the cold window glass,
my grandmother waving a long yellow broom.

Now it comes down again and again,
moves inside the pipes of the house, flutters,
knocks, pounds, the water rising around it,
its head down, body bent down, mouth open,
now closed, trailing a long streamer of paper.

Now there are twenty, thirty piled by the chimney.
I lie down and they come out of my skin,
cover me completely. I pick them up and they dissolve
in my hands—feather and bone, a splinter,
one thin wafer the size of the moon filling the room.

Then they are gone. December, my grandmother
and I sit before the fire and drink tea.
She smoothes the napkin over her thigh,
rattles her saucer, brings the cup to her lips.
This is lovely, I say, *lovely,* a huge white bird in my arms.

III
Let down the Nets

Sea-woman

She sat in the boat, huddled beneath the bow, head down, knees bent, her arms wound around her shins. It was a cool May afternoon and the wind blew along the lake and the sails flapped and her tiny red scarf flapped against her head. She reached up and tightened the knot. Then she pulled me closer and for a moment I too became afraid of the water, of a storm, of tipping the boat over. She never learned how to swim. I wanted to get up, to leave her, to sit in the middle of the boat with my father and brothers. I wanted to guide the rudder, to lower the mast, swing the sails, ropes, leaning my whole body toward the water. But I stayed down there beneath the bow with her.

And she told me stories. In the old days in Ireland, she said, men made small boats from one cow's skin. They stretched the hide over laths and sewed a long seam. The boat was weightless like a basket. It would skim out over the water—the safest thing on the sea. The fishermen in currachs received medals for saving other larger craft caught on the rocks. And in the old days, she said, if you were a bad sinner, they put you in a currach and set you out to sea with no food, water, oars.

And some of these fishermen traced their descent back to the sea-woman. She appeared one day on shore as a seal, took off her skin and became a lovely woman. A young man saw her, stole her skin and she followed him home where he dressed her in ordinary clothes and she forgot about the sea. The young man married her and they had three children and all went well until one day when the youngest child found a strange bundle hidden in the barn and brought it to her mother who recognized her sealskin and remembered her own people and life at sea. Then she said good-bye to her children, put on the skin and slipped under the waves and never again came on land, although she often swam on the surface just off shore, talking and singing to her children.

And each night I sat beside her bed, I wanted to rock her. I wanted to leave her. She called my name and I came to her and she thought me her mother, she thought me her father, the doctor. She called my name and I came to her but I wanted to turn back like a fisherman seeing a red-haired woman on his way to sea. I wanted to stay there beside her and sing to her. I saw myself floating away with her, a sinner, wrapped in her skin.

Folding Up

I slept beside you on this cot,
like your mother during the days
of the white plague, nursing

her brother in a tent pitched
at the foot of Pike's Peak.
At night I listened for your cough.

It swelled. It filled the room,
a red corpuscle, bursting,
pink as baby skin. I dozed

and you called for your mother
again and again and again.
I dreamed her name a needle

slipped into your vein; her blood
hung in a bag over your head.
It became my lantern,

swaying back sixty years.
I saw three women in flames,
fading into one blue morning.

Mother, today I'm folding up
this cot, straightening the corners
of this room. I run my hand over

the window with a cool cloth.
The radiator knocks and steams.
The door closes like a canvas flap.

Currach
for my brother

A picture of you at the beach
lying on the rocks, a rope dangled
over the cliff. You are ten, the camera
focused in on your freckles, your red hair,
the tiny black boat knit into your sweater.

You would put me there in the boat,
and I would be your mother, inside her again,
her smooth skin stretched over ribs.
And you would be an old red-haired woman
walking along the sand, digging up shells
with her toes. And I would be your mother,
afraid of water, of storms, an old red-haired
woman easing me away from the shore, her hand
on my shoulder, her skirt circling her thighs.

Shell

Inside,
the sounds of a frozen lake.
December, and my brother

leans on my arm, his ankles weak,
scraping together as we skate,
first on one foot, the other,

the snow sweeping up,
stinging our eyes.
We glide a cool ten feet.

The ice melts and my brother
rows me out to the middle
of the place, stands up

in the boat, waving, as if
seeing someone on shore.
The boat flips and I hang

onto the bar, my head
bobbing above the water
into the boat's chamber.

And now the ribs
of that boat settle down,
become the arched beams

of this ceiling, a chapel.
Inside, a priest saying Mass,
a nuptial, and someone leans

on my brother's arm as he
walks down the aisle. Flowers
falling on the carpet, whiten,

harden, break under foot.
He reaches the back of the
church, puts his ear to the door.

Outside,
the sounds of the wind
blowing someone across the lake.

In a Dream

It floats toward you:
a mother, a fish,
something without breath,
shiny, washed smooth
as the skin of a leech.

It is young, cool.
You feel it diving into you,
lodge between muscle and bone,
move one spiny fin.
Your whole body goes numb.

A pink stain spreads
across the surface of the sea
as if underneath
something invisible
boiled or bled.

It is your mother's yellow
finger pressed into stone,
her hand cracked open,
flesh stripped away,
half-eaten.

It is your mother's arm
wrapped around you,
tangled in yours, one,
two tentacles crossing,
beating one breast.

It is your own hand
reaching for hers,
drawing her in
like water through gills,
sifting, settling,

her bones in your lungs,
her whole body growing
inside yours, pulling
you downward to a
pillow, a bed of coral.

November

1

The wind drives through
the field to the house.
Up on the hill,
a woman moves from
the house to the yard,
her arms loaded with
wet laundry. She stands
at the line, her children
gathered around her,
sitting on the ground.
Over their heads, the white
sheets flap like sails.
A combine moves across
the field, rocking,
steaming, full of
immigrants. The woman
stands at the rail,
her skirt blowing upwards.
Her face is gone.
It is the land.
It is the ground
under her feet
where she drops her
children one by one.
The wind shakes the trees
and the woman moves back
into the house, through
the door marked with
two ears of corn.
It is November and

there is a daughter
standing in the yard,
the woman's eyes closing,
sinking into her own face,
the woman's garden,
the plants rising
from the ground,
spread out before her
like a fine Irish linen.

2

Everything is green,
is brown: the daughter
standing in the field,
moving along the rows,
the woman behind her,
chopping corn, her knife
as long as her arm, her legs
wrapped in newspaper.
Her skin is light, thin
and the papers rustle
as she walks. She walks
into the house. She wads
the paper and lights
the stove. The water boils.
The season is open,
the turnips, the squash
picked, stacked in the

cellar where the woman
sits on the floor
with a mound of pheasant.
One feather, two,
she pulls the roots
from the skin, she pulls
the bird inside out,
spreading its wings,
and there are the
intestines, the liver,
the heart, wrapped in
a piece of paper.
It is November
and the woman stands
in the kitchen slicing
meat. The men lean into
the counter, drinking,
talking about the wind,
the crops. The daughter
is in the corner by the
stove. The water boils.
The woman sits in the
next room, in the parlor
and stares into the mirror.
She sees her face
in shadow, her arms
folded into her lap.

3

The season is open
and there is a daughter
standing in the yard.
She watches the house.
She watches the woman
inside the house move
toward the window, run
her hand through her hair.
The woman turns on the light
and her face floats over
the ceiling, the lamp.
The season is open
and there is a daughter
standing in the light
by the window. She steps
out of the room,
out of the house.
It is November,
the sky cool, clear.
The fir trees brush
her face as she walks.
She walks across the field
toward the pond where
the ice forms a bridge.
She crosses.
She crosses it again,
the wind behind her.
Every door is open
and when she comes
home the woman is

standing in the kitchen
lighting the stove.
It is dawn.
The woman stamps
her feet on the floor.
The daughter stares out
the window and the hill
is a white sheet folding.

Manning, Iowa

Song

And each night was a vigil:
the moon, the two small candles beside your bed, the only light.
And the wicks burning, traveling through your body, the needle,
the long strings, the green mold boring a hole through the bread.

And the wax melting, the thin wax lips taking you in, the hollow,
the cup, your lung filling, draining . . .

And the flames rising, hanging in the air, were tongues
inside bells ringing the hours: one, one;
tongues inside your body when I was there.

And the moon, rising over your bed, was a host.
And your body was eaten.

Succession

It doesn't matter if the light fails.
Tonight, my fingers move automatically
Along the rows, each stitch
As familiar as a bead of the rosary.

I simply follow the family pattern
My Irish grandmothers knit into sweaters
For their sons, the fine threads
Spun off the skulls of Nordic sailors.

And when I stop to raise my hands,
It will be in the way of a priest
Blessing boats. I'll poke my arms
Through the dark and listen

For the clack of needles, oars.
I'll prostrate myself on the floor,
Let down the nets, the great walls
Of the house, and float out,

The tides, the full moon, a tangle
Of yarn, pulling me in, cell by cell,
My flesh unraveling, all revealing
Marks gone: scars, face, fingerprints,

My whole body the shore by dawn.